The Rules to Be Cool

Etiquette and Netiquette

Karla Dougherty

Enslow Publishers, Inc.

40 Industrial Road   PO Box 38
Box 398   Aldershot
Berkeley Heights, NJ 07922   Hants GU12 6BP
USA   UK

http://www.enslow.com

Acknowledgment

With thanks to:

Judith Ré, author of *Social Savvy: A Teenager's Guide to Feeling Confident in Any Situation,* for her review of this book.

Library of Congress Cataloging-in-Publication Data

Dougherty, Karla.
    The rules to be cool : etiquette and netiquette /Karla Dougherty.
        p. cm.
    Includes bibliographical references and index.
    Contents: Why be polite? — Home front — School rules — Public scenes — The social scene — Netiquette.
    ISBN 0-7660-1607-2
    1. Etiquette for children and teenagers—Juvenile literature.
    [1. Etiquette.] I. Title.

    BJ1857.C5 D68 2001
    395.1'23—dc21   00-010311
                                                CIP

Printed in the United States of America

10 9 8 7 6 5 4 3 2

To Our Readers: We have done our best to make sure all Internet addresses in this book were active and appropriate when we went to press. However, the author and the publisher have no control over and assume no liability for the material available on those Internet sites or on other Web sites they may link to. Any comments or suggestions can be sent by e-mail to comments@enslow.com or to the address on the back cover.

Illustration credits: © Corel Corporation pp. 8, 37, 53; Fran Pelzman Liscio, pp. 16, 21, 29, 42, 44.

Cover illustration: © Skjold photos; Background © Corel Corporation.

Contents

1

Why Be Polite?

Dear Suzy Social:

My friends and I were at a basketball game last week. During halftime a group of kids from the other school followed us out to the hallway. They started laughing and making fun of us. They even threw popcorn at the back of our heads! My friends felt really bad and wanted to fight back, but I said we should ignore them. My friends called me a scaredy cat. Who was right?

Signed: Maybe Not So Scaredy Cat

Dear Not So:

Let me be the first to applaud you! You not only were NOT a coward, but you showed excellent manners—and you might even have stopped a fight from getting out of hand! The kids from the other school were boorish (that means rude) and boring. Why join them in their poor attitude? By ignoring them, you proved that you were bigger—and cooler—than all of them put together. Bravo!

Signed: Suzy Social

Dear Suzy Social:

I had to write to you about this kid who really made a difference in my first week at a new school. I was brand-new that first day, and, because I'm kind of taller and heavier than most teens, I was really nervous that I'd be laughed at—which usually happens to me. Well, sure enough, as I walked down the hall, the kids standing by their lockers started pointing at me and whispering. A couple of them started laughing. Well, I just hugged my books and kept my head low, like I always do, feeling miserable and fighting back tears, when this kid came over to me and said a great big hi. She smiled and took me to my first class and, as she walked, she gave the other kids dirty looks and ignored their comments. She even met me for lunch in the cafeteria. Thanks to her, the kids stopped picking on me. I was accepted. I wanted other kids to know about this— because I have a feeling that this is what etiquette is all about: being kind.

Signed: New Kid on the Block

Dear New Kid:

Thank you so much for your letter! It so clearly showed the difference a little kindness can make. People think that etiquette is all about knowing what fork to use and not burping at the table. Certainly, those things are important to the enjoyment of a meal, but etiquette is much more than that. It is all about being kind and helpful to others—just as you would want them to be to you. Think of it as an investment: the more manners you use, the more you will get back. I'm glad you are settled in your new school. And remember: Someone else will be new next term, so do not forget to take him or her under your wing!

Signed: Suzy Social

Etiquette, to most people, does not go beyond please and thank you, using a knife and fork, and sending "thank you" cards for presents. But as these letters to Suzy Social show, good etiquette can create a happy atmosphere. It can make everyone—friends, family members, and new classmates—feel good.

Good manners got a stodgy reputation during the 1960s, when "let it all hang out" was the credo for teens. The idea that manners were old-fashioned lasted through the 1970s and manners got an even worse reputation in the 1980s. As Linda Hill, a consultant with the Colorado School of Protocol and Etiquette in Denver, Colorado, said, "People somehow embraced the theory that if you have enough money, you can be as obnoxious as you want to be."[1]

But now, as the new century begins, nice is back. It is nice to be nice, to be considerate. This new trend toward

The Random House Dictionary of the English Language defines etiquette as "conventional requirements as to social behavior; properties of conduct as established in any class or community or for any occasion."[2] In less "proper" terms, this means that there is a code of behavior that makes any situation better. Etiquette is a way of separating us from other animals. It is a part of civilized society—and helps keep mean, nasty words and actions away.

Learning the rules of fine dining can improve a teen's self-esteem. At a simple table setting, the fork is set on the left. The napkin also goes on the left. The knife and teaspoon are set to the right of the plate.

manners and consideration is a boon for everyone, including teenagers who might need to feel more comfortable in unfamiliar territory (such as starting the first year in high school or asking a new friend to go out for a soda).[3] And, if teens feel more comfortable, their nerves will calm down and, even better, they will get a dose of confidence.

There is more. Manners are a sign of civilized society. They can help lead to a better way of life. Ethene Jones, an ordained minister, works with children from Dallas, Texas. She takes them out to dinner or to a movie to teach them how to act in a social situation. "If you can eat in fine restaurants, you learn a new way to carry yourself, and that improves your self-esteem," Ms. Jones told *The Dallas Morning News*. "I always felt that if I learned how to carry myself, I could eat with the president if I wanted to."[4]

In short, good manners teach people how to act as they make their way into the world. They can help young people communicate with others, be respectful, and be respected themselves.[5]

2

Home Front

Dear Suzy Social:

My younger sister is always borrowing my expensive shampoo. I love her and do not want to say no, but the last time I went to use my shampoo, it was empty! My sister had used the whole thing and never told me. That was it. I told her she couldn't borrow my things anymore. We started to fight and my mother ended up getting mad at both of us. Boy, was I steamed! Am I being selfish?

Signed: Wet Head

Dear Wet Head:

Your first impulse was a good one. Being generous to those you love is a wonderful thing. The trouble occurs when generosity is not clearly stated. When you offered your shampoo, you should have spelled out the rules: Tell me when the bottle is used up. Sometimes you cannot count on others to remember to be considerate. You have to spell things out—especially if a younger sibling is involved. The best solution? Tell your little sister she is welcome to use your shampoo, but she must tell you when she has used the last drop. And let your mother know that you have worked things out. She will be very proud of you!

Signed: Suzy Social

Learning good manners starts long before the teen years. Little children discover early on the "magic" of words such as "please" and "thank you." When a child says "please" before asking for a cookie, he stands a much better chance of getting one. When she says "thank you," her mother smiles. It does not take long to realize that being polite has its rewards—and not just in sweets. The use of good manners can make the whole atmosphere at home more pleasant.[1]

"People judge you by your manners, whether you like it or not," says Ann Nicol, a former staff assistant to several ambassadors at the United States Mission to the United Nations and the founder of Nicol Associates, an etiquette consulting firm. "Good manners are a habit. When you act correctly without thinking about it, it helps you as a person. You will have an easier time of it in life. And the quicker you learn good manners, the faster they will become a part of you."[2]

Learning those good manners, starting with those "magic words" parents teach their children, begins at home. Here are some of the situations that call for good manners "on the family front."

"Please Pass the Peas," or Dinner Table Manners

The kitchen or dining room at home is not meant to be a formal place. Mealtime with the family is when a person can unwind and relax. But informal does not have to mean rude. Eating with the family can be a better experience for everyone if a teenager simply learns to **EAT**:

- **E**tiquette at the dinner table is easy. Teens just need to follow proper table manners. Teens can set an example for younger siblings (and make parents proud) by following some basic rules, such as placing a napkin on their laps, not talking with their mouths full, keeping their elbows off the table, and placing used utensils on the side of their plates.

- **A**sk questions, listen, and speak up. In other words, turn off the television or put down that book—and talk. Teens can fill the void by asking how their parents' days were, how a younger brother and sister did in school, or by volunteering information about themselves. They might even be surprised at the encouragement and support they receive in return for their good behavior.

- **T**reat all family members with respect. This means saying please and thank you when passing food, asking to be excused, and showing appreciation for a delicious meal when dinner is finished.[3]

Teenagers in Etiquette History

As much as the rules of good manners may make teenagers groan, things were a lot harder in medieval England. In middle-class families up to the sixteenth century, a teen would have been sent to live with a different family to learn polite behavior. A boy would have been a manservant and a girl, a maid-in-waiting, working for another family for several months or years. English households believed that children were better able to learn about manners and discipline away from home.[4]

"Leave Me Alone!" or Respecting Privacy

Two teenage boys, Zack Elias and Travis Goldman, had a lot to say about privacy and being a teenager. In fact, they published a humor book called *How Not to Embarrass Your Kids*. In it, they offer some funny suggestions to parents, all of them on the same theme.

- Do not ask.
- Do not pretend to be looking through a child's backpack for paper and pen.
- Do not ever come into a teenager's bedroom without knocking.[5]

These rules might be written in jest, but there is truth behind the jokes. Teenagers need as much privacy as their parents.

Knowing that is half the battle. If a teen knows she wants to be alone in her bedroom, she can put herself in her parents' place and see that they might need some time alone as well. She will realize that maybe she should not enter their bedroom without knocking first.[6]

It is only a short walk from her parents' bedroom to her siblings' rooms. Maybe her brother and sister feel the same way. Maybe she should not tease her brother when he is quietly studying. Maybe she should not rummage through her sister's closet when her sister is on the phone. Ask first.

Privacy. It is an important part of self-respect—and respecting others. A little consideration on the home front can translate into success in the outside world. Kindness is contagious—and welcome.

Here are some consideration issues—and advice on how to handle them:

- *Bathroom manners.* Most teenagers have to share a bathroom, sometimes with the entire family, sometimes with a brother or sister. But sharing means, well, sharing—of time, counter space, and products. If more than one person has to leave the house at the same time in the morning, no one should "hog" the bathroom. Sinks and showers should be kept clean. Dirty towels should be put in the hamper.

- *Timing is everything.* Life would be perfect if family members were always available to each other. If a teen wanted an answer to a homework question right now, his father would get off the phone. If a teen wanted to ask her brother a question about school, she could knock and enter his room without hesitation. If parents asked their children to turn off the television, the remote would be clicked off without argument. Unfortunately, life does not work that way. People do not always do what others want, the instant it is desired. Parents have to be sensitive to their children—and children have to be sensitive to their parents.[7]

○ *A chore is a chore.* No doubt about it. Doing the dishes, taking out the garbage, or making the bed is not fun. There is a reason why these activities are called "chores." But everyone has to pitch in sometimes. Clothes and bedrooms and dishes are not cleaned by magic. For a house to run smoothly and peacefully, everyone has to pitch in. In the time it takes to complain about taking out the garbage, it could already be outside in the bin.

○ *Phone friend.* The telephone is so much a part of all our lives that sometimes it feels as if the receiver grows out of our ears. But telephones are more than a way to keep up with friends. They can be a way to communicate important messages. In fact, learning how to use the phone is one of the first business skills a young adult needs in the "real world." Some tips include:

   ✓ *Speak clearly.* Do not chew gum while trying to talk.

   ✓ *When making a call, the teenager should ask if this is a good time to talk.* It might be better to call back later.

   ✓ *Be polite.* Do not answer the phone with a growl of annoyance. Even if you

When using the phone, speak clearly. Get off the phone politely if another family member needs to make a call.

do not recognize the voice or the name of the person on the other end, say hello and good-bye—using the person's name if you know it.

✓ *Take messages down carefully.* Always write messages down and, if possible, record the time of the call. Repeat names and numbers to make sure they are correct.

✓ *Never say "I am home alone."* Instead, teens should always say that their mother or father is unable to come to the phone. They should never offer personal information, either.[8]

✓ *If "call waiting" clicks on, a teen should say, "Excuse me, the other line is ringing."* He should tell the new caller that he is on the other line and will call back (or take a message for the person being called). He should then immediately click back to the first caller and say, "I'm sorry for the interruption," and continue to chat—unless he really has to take the second call. Then he needs to say exactly that—politely. [9]

Home Rules: A Top Ten List

Harmony, peace, and even fun are not impossible at home. Follow these simple rules of etiquette, and anyone, at any age, may find home a good place to be.

Number 10: Answer the phone politely and write messages down.

Number 9: Dry the dishes or take out the garbage without whining.

Number 8: Try to make conversation at the dinner table.

Number 7: Keep bathrooms clean.

Number 6: Do not hog the bathroom.

Number 5: Watch, look, and listen before "bothering" someone. Ask if it is a good time to talk.

Number 4: Use table manners at dinner.

Number 3: Be polite. Saying please and thank you only takes a second and makes the other person feel good.

Number 2: Do not use things that do not belong to you without asking. This includes shampoo, notebooks, CDs, and clothes.

And the *Number 1* rule of home life?

Show respect and consideration for all the members of the family.

3

School Rules

Dear Suzy Social:

Something happened in geography class this week that embarrassed me a lot. My teacher was talking about rock formation while my best friend passed me a note. I was not listening to a word he said. I was too busy reading! Suddenly, the teacher called a pop quiz. I was so upset that I said a swear word. The teacher got mad at me and told me that I would be punished for my rudeness—by having to wash the blackboards after school. My classmates started laughing and snickering at me. I didn't mean to create a scene, but what else could I do? I really wanted to read the note!

Signed: Confused in Geography

Dear Confused in Geography:

Imagine if the scene you described was played out a little differently:

It's the same geography class, with the same classmates and teacher. He's talking about rock formation again and you would much rather read that note you just received. But you know this teacher has a reputation for pop quizzes. Plus you also know that there is only half an hour left to the class and you could read the note later. Instead of ignoring the lesson, you listen—and you are ready for the pop quiz. You are not rude and you do not say something you will be sorry for after class. You mouth, "Later," to your best friend, who, of course understands. All is well and you might even ace the quiz!

The moral of my story? Proper behavior not only helps make other people feel better, it can help you do better in school!

Signed: Suzy Social

Teenagers know what is expected of them at school almost from the very first day they say good-bye to their parents and enter the classroom. They know they have to get their homework in on time and show up for class—and not read a friend's note in class.

But, as every teenager also knows, there is a lot more to school than schoolwork. There are the other kids, the peer pressure that is so strong it can be hard to resist. Teenagers

"In order for a teenager to become successful in the outside world, to have a happy, fulfilled adult life, he or she needs to know about respect. How to receive it—and how to give it," says Dr. Steven Dranoff, a clinical psychologist who has organized programs on respect for students in schools across the country. "Respect can be learned."[1]

Try to follow the golden rule at school—Do Unto Others as You Would Have Them Do Unto You—that means treating your schoolmates with respect.

want to be accepted by their peers. They want to be liked—or at least respected.

One way to get respect is to have respect for oneself. Make friends with people who are supportive and accepting, and who may also share the same interests. Do not try to be friends with the popular kids—just because they are popular.

In general, try to follow the Golden Rule: Do Unto Others as You Would Have Them Do Unto You. This means that people should treat other people the way they want to be treated themselves. If a teen wants people to smile at her, she should plant a smile on her face. If a teen wants a compliment, he should give one to someone else. If a teen wants help with her homework, she should help someone else with a different assignment.

"Respect is also learning right from wrong," says Dr. Dranoff. "If you have no values, chances are you will not give people the respect they are due. Nor will you like yourself too much."[2]

In an example Dr. Dranoff uses in his school programs, a boy and a girl are discussing a party that is being planned for that night. The girl is not sure if she is going; none of her friends can make it. But the boy knows that the party was set up so that the girl would be alone with some guys. He does not know what to do. If he tells her about the plan, he would be ratting on his friends. But if he does not? The girl will be set up for a potential disaster.

One answer is clear: The situation has to be prevented. But how? Perhaps the boy can tell his friends that what they are doing is wrong—and avoid having to rat on them. Or perhaps a few girlfriends can go to the party with the girl, providing "safety in numbers." Or the boy can just warn the girl outright and take whatever consequences there are.[3]

There are several approaches to the right answer, but whichever one the boy chooses, he will have gained a sense of respect.

- The courage to do the right thing gives him self-respect.

- Being considerate of his peers gives him their respect ("Do Unto Others" Golden Rule).

- Learning respect gives him a real sense of what is right and what is wrong. He has learned values—without having to take a class in how to do so.

When Is a Nerd Not a Nerd?

As the 1999 NBC television program *Freaks and Geeks* showed, being geeky is not necessarily a bad thing. One of the main characters on the show, a geek, managed to win the admiration of the most popular cheerleader in the high school.

Was it the power of the tube? Partially. But the motivation remains the same, whether in a script or in real life. The geek won the cheerleader's friendship by being considerate, friendly, and helpful.

Here are some other nerdy moves that might not seem cool by some classmates' standards, but will surely win the admiration of others.

Good Manners in the Hall

It is hard to find the logic in slamming a door in someone's face or stepping all over papers that fell out of a locker. It makes much more sense—and adds to a teen's confidence and self-respect—to help a classmate pick up his scattered papers, open a door for a teacher or student loaded down

Teacher's Pet . . . Peeve

Manners do begin at home—and they carry over into the classroom. Students have to remember that teachers are people, too. They do not like to be interrupted or criticized. They do not care for students who hog the floor and ask personal questions. If there is anything on a teenager's mind, he should ask to speak to his teacher in private—when it is convenient for the teacher. Issues might include anything from a teacher not pronouncing a teen's name correctly to a student's request for a makeup test.[4]

with books, or make room at a crowded cafeteria table where there do not seem to be any seats left. And what teen or teacher would not like a student to do these polite things?

School Rules: A Top Ten List

All teens have to do is follow these basic "ABCs of etiquette" and they will not only do well in school, but also in the real world.

Number 10: Do not interrupt a teacher when she is talking.

Number 9: Be helpful: Open doors and help retrieve dropped papers.

Number 8: Never tease or make fun of anyone. How would you like it if someone teased you?

Number 7: Make the first day at a new school feel like an adventure.

Number 6: Be considerate of other classmates.

Number 5: Timing is as important in school as at home. Teens should find out the best time to talk to teachers—not blurt out private information in class.

Number 4: When there is a problem, think of a solution. Instead of not being prepared for a test and feeling the pressure to cheat, a teen can do his homework and zip through the quiz.

Number 3: Try to make friends with others who have the same values.

Number 2: Obey school rules: Do your homework and come to class on time.

And the *Number 1* rule of school days?

Treat each other with mutual respect.

4

Public Scenes

Dear Readers:

I came across these old-fashioned rules of etiquette and thought I would pass them along. After reading them, I am sure you will be glad you live in today's world instead of long ago!

"At a ball or evening-party a hostess should receive her guests at the head of the staircase, and should remain there until the majority, if not all, of the guests have arrived." [1]

"When a lady arrives at the Palace she should leave her wraps in the cloak-room with one of the maids in attendance." [2]

"A man should never come down to breakfast barefoot. Nothing will do but walking shoes or boots." [3]

"For older boys and girls from fourteen to eighteen years of age, tennis tournaments in the summer and hockey matches in the

winter are usually considered . . . suitable entertainments. A substantial tea is given after a hockey match."[4]

These pearls of advice on good manners were written by a member of the British aristocracy in the early part of the twentieth century. They sound silly now, and certainly out-of-date and out of touch. But are they?

Even though palace etiquette and greeting guests at a ball are not situations encountered today, the basic rules of etiquette still apply. Today's teens might not have spiral staircases or at-home hockey games and certainly few of them will ever get to meet a queen, but the message then and now is still clear: Act in a civilized fashion. In other words, be polite and gracious at a party, an outing, or, yes, even when curtseying to a queen.

Teen Diplomacy

When people venture out in public, they are going to be around others. A movie star really has to watch what she says and does because it will become news in the next day's papers. But regular teenagers? They might not have to say no to that delicious dessert. They can even wear their favorite jeans with the holes in the knees. But if they act in a rude fashion—throwing food in a restaurant, talking and laughing out loud at the movies, or heckling the other team at a sports event—it will get noticed. And more times than not, the result will not just be a dirty look. The penalties might include embarrassment, a hefty fine, and an unwelcome punishment from mom and dad.

But teens do not have to stay indoors with the shades drawn and the doors locked. Here are some simple hints to help teens everywhere, in every city and every state, to be the best they can be when they are out in public.

Public Places #1: Follow Their Lead

Sam hated it when his mother told him to put his napkin on his lap or when she made him set the table for dinner. He was not happy when she checked his fingernails and made him wash up before they ate. He wished she would just leave him alone. Who cared about these formalities? But one day he was invited to a party given by a friend he had made that summer in camp. It was a very formal affair; there was even a celebrity there. All of a sudden Sam was glad his mother had told him which fork to use when. He was glad she made sure his nails were clean and that he had learned how to make conversation. Without the manners he had learned at home, Sam would not only have felt more ill at ease, but he would also have been very embarrassed.

Contrary to popular teenage folklore, parents are not always stupid. Sometimes they really know something that a teenager does not. They have lived longer and they have experienced much more than a thirteen-year-old.

True, the older a teen gets, the more he sees his parents as people. When he was a little kid, he saw his parents as wiser and so much older than himself. But, as he grows, he realizes his parents are people, too. They have strengths and weaknesses just like everyone else. Unfortunately, seeing those weaknesses for the first time can upset a teen. He cannot understand why his parents are cranky or irritable—and, in reaction, he gets cranky, too.[5]

Public Places #2: The Thou Shalt Nots

Linda and a friend were trying to watch the new Leonardo Di Caprio movie, but the group of teens in front of them kept shouting and laughing and throwing popcorn at each other. She wanted to say something, but she recognized the teens from school. She was too embarrassed to ask the manager to quiet them down and she did not want to draw attention to herself by moving her seat. She was afraid the rude teens would start shouting at her. Instead, she suffered in silence, fuming.

Royce brought his date to a neighborhood Italian restaurant. He was excited and pleased; it was his first date and he liked the girl he was with very much. But by the time they ordered their spaghetti and sodas, the mood was ruined—thanks to two teenage couples sitting in the booth behind them. They were shouting and telling dirty jokes; Royce could barely hear a word his date said. He was so embarrassed. The other teens were ruining his night. He had to ask the waitress to change their seats.

These scenarios are very common and, like Linda and Royce, there probably is not a teen anywhere who has not been on the receiving end of a rude teenager.

By sheer experience, parents still know more than their kids. They know about manners and polite behavior. Teens need to listen to their parents when they tell them to hush in the movies; when they make them use a knife and fork; when they ask them to drink milk from a glass, not from the carton; and when they smile as they introduce someone new. Listen and learn.

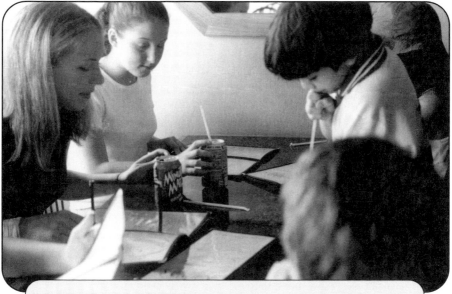

It is hard to order food, or even to look at a menu carefully, when someone nearby is slurping his drink.

Etiquette can make life easier for everyone. It can help teens and adults alike view a movie in silence, browse through an art exhibit or a store, enjoy a restaurant meal, and study without interruption. Some of the most important "shalt nots" of public places include:

- *Do not yell.* Remember that public means that other people will be around. People are not alone as they would be at home. Whether in a restaurant, a hall, a store, or a movie theater, teens—and all people—should keep their voices down.[6]

- *Do not stare.* No matter how strange someone's outfit or hair color is, do not stare at them.[7]

▭ *Do not forget to say please and thank you.* These words not only open doors, they should be said when doors are opened. These two words should also be used when a waiter serves food, when a salesperson helps a teen find the perfect pair of jeans, and when someone makes room on a crowded bus.[8]

▭ *Do not push, jostle, or bump another person.* When on an elevator, a crowded street, an escalator, or waiting in line, try to avoid contact with others.[9]

▭ *Do not ignore the words "excuse me."* Whether it is an accidental bump or a loud sneeze (with mouth covered, please), the phrase is always appreciated.

▭ *Do not get ahead of anyone in line.* The only exception? If a teen urgently needs to use the restroom or is late for a bus or train, she can ask permission of the people in front of her by politely saying, "Excuse me. May I go ahead of you? It's an emergency." And, of course, no one should forget to say thank you when allowed to move to the front of the line.[10]

▭ *Do not be late.* True, sometimes it is inevitable. There are situations that make people late: traffic, emergencies at home, a broken-down car. But, whenever possible, teenagers should leave their house or school in enough time to get where they have to go. If it is a new place in a new town, even more time should be given to get to a place on time. The worst case scenario? Getting there early and having to shop or browse in a mall.

⊘ *Do not treat people with disabilities differently in public or in private.* They are not "special" or needy. If they want help, they will ask for it. They do not want to feel like heroes. They only want to feel equal.[11]

Public Policy: A Top Ten List

With good manners, teenagers can be proud ambassadors of their home, family, and school. They can go anywhere and do anything with style and poise. And, by not having to worry about how to act in strange surroundings, they can relax and have a better time. All this with just ten simple rules to remember:

Number 10: Do not talk in the movies.

Number 9: Speak softly (do not yell) when dining out or shopping in a mall.

Number 8: Do not litter—anywhere.

Number 7: Say please and thank you as often as needed.

Number 6: Try not to jostle, bump, or push people on the street or on an elevator or escalator.

Number 5: If a bump is unavoidable, do not forget to say excuse me.

Number 4: Do not stare—ever!

Number 3: Remember, public means public: Teens should not "scratch where it itches," use dental floss, or act in any way that would make others uncomfortable.

Number 2: People with disabilities are exactly that: people. Do not treat them in any special fashion—unless asked.

And the *Number 1* rule of public places?

Believe it or not, parents know what they are talking about. Listen. Watch. Follow their lead.

5

The Social Scene

Dear Suzy Social:

There's a guy who really likes me but I do not like him. I always see him at school and parties and things and he always wants to monopolize my time. I do not want to hurt his feelings, but I do not want to lead him on either. What can I do about it?

Signed: Confused

Dear Confused:

You show a great deal of sensitivity, which is one of the first rules of good manners. Rejection is never easy, whether you are the one doing it or receiving it. In this case, the best solution is honesty—but with sensitivity. Tell your friend that you like him very much but not as a boyfriend. It will hurt at first, but the boy will be much better off finding someone who will appreciate him more.[1]

Dear Suzy Social:

Some of the kids in our school call us a clique. But we have never seen ourselves like that. We are just a group of kids who like to hang out together. There is a girl in our school who keeps trying to be with us. She is always around. On one level, I am flattered. People tell us we are the most popular group in school. But on another level, she is really becoming a nuisance. We have tried ignoring her, but it just does not seem to work. What should we do?

Signed: Fed Up

Dear Fed Up:

Actually, the girl who is the outsider should be the one fed up! You have forgotten the Golden Rule of Etiquette: Do Unto Others as You Would Have Them Do Unto You. Wouldn't you feel bad if someone ignored you?! Cliques are often created because the people in them do not have enough self-esteem within themselves to be independent. You and your friends might look like the best and the brightest, but maybe it is because you have all worked so hard to convince yourselves. Maybe it is time to expand your horizons, meet new people, and hear what others have to say. You never know. You just might find yourself with a good friend for life![2]

Dear Suzy Social:

One of my best friends always wears the wrong clothes. Either her pants are too tight or her sweaters too baggy. What is worse is she thinks she looks fabulous—and she always asks me if I agree! Should I just ignore her taste in clothes or should I be honest and say something?

Signed: Fashionista

Dear Fashionista:

This is a tricky situation. You want to be honest, but you do not want to hurt your friend's feelings either. It is really your friend's business how she dresses, but impressions count and her clothes may hurt her chances out in the real world. The good news is you can be both honest and sensitive. The next time she asks you how she looks, mix some kindness with your truth. Tell her the baggy sweater does not show off her nice figure. Tell her the pants do not fit her as well as some others in her closet. Offer to go shopping with her—and make a fun day of it. (And remember: It is her day. Do not end up looking for clothes for yourself!) [3]

These letters give examples of very common situations that affect kids every day. The fact is that the "social graces"—meeting and greeting people, being able to carry on a conversation, being polite, and using tact to get out of sticky situations—are all things a teen can carry through his or her whole life.

By knowing how to act at get-togethers, at a neighbor's house, at a party, or on a date, teens will find themselves not only popular, but with an advantage in starting a career and embarking on life after high school. "First impressions are made in only five seconds," says teenage etiquette expert Ann Nicol. "That's all you have to make a good impression on someone, whether that person is a teacher, a friend's parent, someone you want to know better, or, later, an employer or college administrator."[4]

Luckily, first impressions can be changed. But, rather than being forced to undo a bad impression, teenagers can easily learn how to put their best foot forward with poise and confidence. And, as an added plus, they can not only make a lasting good impression, but also one that is

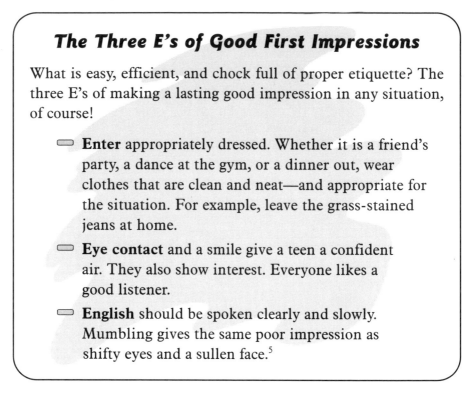

The Three E's of Good First Impressions

What is easy, efficient, and chock full of proper etiquette? The three E's of making a lasting good impression in any situation, of course!

- **Enter** appropriately dressed. Whether it is a friend's party, a dance at the gym, or a dinner out, wear clothes that are clean and neat—and appropriate for the situation. For example, leave the grass-stained jeans at home.

- **Eye contact** and a smile give a teen a confident air. They also show interest. Everyone likes a good listener.

- **English** should be spoken clearly and slowly. Mumbling gives the same poor impression as shifty eyes and a sullen face.[5]

respectful, sensitive, and responsible to others. Acting like this can make a good time even better. Not a bad deal at all!

The Social Whirl

Human beings are social animals. We all need to interact with other people, to laugh, cry, and share the good times and bad. Teenagers, especially, with their need to become independent of their parents, count on their friends to help them along.[6]

And action, any action, speaks louder than words. A teen could have the three E's down pat—speaking clearly, wearing appropriate clothes, and smiling—but if he starts

First impressions are often lasting ones. To make sure the first impression is a good one, put on a clean face, neat hair and clothes, and a smile.

to drink and cause a ruckus, no one is going to remember his smile or his nice shirt.

Similarly, if a teen starts to clean off the table after dinner at a friend's house—and she has *also* dressed appropriately and been polite during the meal—there is no question that her first impression is not only a good one, but also a long-lasting solid one.

Acting politely and with consideration does not mean a teen cannot have a good time. Quite the opposite. It means not having to think about how he appears to others. It means relaxing and enjoying himself. It means he will be welcome back any time.

Here are some of the social whirls—and how to handle them—that teenagers will find themselves in at one time or another during their school years.

Social Whirl #1: We Are Going to Have a Party!

In ancient Egypt, party guests donned perfumed wax cone hats when they entered a host's home. As the night wore on in the sultry hot Egyptian air, the hats melted, perfuming one and all.

In the Middle Ages, guests would be licking their fingers after enjoying the wild boar, pigeons, ducks, rabbits, and venison (complete with heads and tails) they ate with their hands—all washed down with fermented ale.

After dinner in the nineteenth century, the hostess and her female guests would be required to leave the room, while the host and his male friends sat alone at the table enjoying brandy and cigars.

Happily, there is no such party etiquette today. When a teenager wants to have a party, she can forget cooking wild beasts, perfuming hats, and leaving the table when she is not ready. All she has to do is get permission from her parents and then plan for it.

But planning takes time and should be done well in advance. The first step? Sending out invitations about one month before the party. A good invitation should include:

- *The kind of party the teen is having.* For example, is it a birthday party or an end of school party for the start of summer?

- *The Who, When, and Where.* Who is giving the party? What is the date? And where will it be held?

- *Extra information.* If a teen is having a swim party, it is a good idea for her to write that guests should bring a swimsuit and a towel. For any party, include information such as that her parents will drive everyone home. It would be especially important to inform guests if the party is a surprise.

- *RSVP.* This is a shortcut for the French phrase, *répondez s'il vous plait.* It means "reply, please." Here, the teen should put her phone number and, if necessary, a date to reply by.

- *Mailings.* Teens should always mail invitations to their friends' homes. They should *never* hand out invitations at school. There is always the chance that someone who is not invited will see the teen handing out invitations to others and be terribly hurt. Avoid such problems by using the U.S. Post Office.[7]

Teens should talk over party plans with their parents.

Together, they can work out a budget, plan the menu and the decorations, figure out how much food to buy, and decide on entertainment. Maybe a teen wants a disc jockey (if the budget allows). Maybe there is someone in town who can read palms. Maybe one teen wants burgers, while another wants snack food like chips and pretzels. Maybe one teen wants balloons, and another wants flowers. And if it is a birthday, there is the all-important cake that must be ordered or baked in advance.

When the day or evening of the party arrives, the host or hostess should be ready at least half an hour before the party so she can make sure all is well. She should be standing by the door, ready to greet guests as they arrive—and make them comfortable.[8]

Some good host openers include:

"Hi! I am so glad you could come. Let me take your coat. Everyone's downstairs."

"Hey. It is good to see you! Do you know Jacob? He likes Smashing Pumpkins too."

"Hello, Madeline. I'm so glad you are here. This is for me? Oh, thank you. That is so sweet. What would you like to drink? Soda or juice?"

A good host circulates during her party. She makes sure guests are having a good time. Here are some hints for the host:

- *If a shy guest is standing by himself,* bring him over to a group of outgoing people and introduce him.

- *Break the ice* by telling guests interesting facts about each other, such as the trip one took to Europe last year, the great tennis player another is, the volunteer work a third does at the hospital.

- *Enlist the help of one or two good friends* to make sure there is enough food and drink on the table and to start chatting with people who seem to be quiet.

- *Parents need to be chaperones* —and they play an important role in a party. They may stay upstairs, out of sight, but they are there just in case there is a problem. Some unforeseen difficulties could include an uninvited guest who refuses to leave, a fight starting, someone who brings alcohol, or the need to dash to the supermarket to restock the party.[9]

When the party is over, the work is not done. Just because a hostess is left with dirty plates and glasses does not mean it has to be a downer, though. The best solution for a teen (and to give mom and dad a break) is to ask one or two friends to help clean up; the friends can talk about the party while they clean. Make it a slumber party, and the fun can last until the next day.[10]

Social Whirl # 2: All Dressed and Ready for a Party!

It is time to turn the tables. Instead of being the teenager giving the party, the would-be hostess has been invited to her friend's house for a slumber party. Being a guest might not have the same responsibilities as being the hostess, but there are certain rules of behavior just the same.

- *Remember that teenage diplomacy?* Whether it is a public place or a friend's house, a teenager is a representative of her home. She should treat her friend's property with respect, and she should respect the privacy of the members of the family. It is always in good

Dear Laura,
    Thank you so much for the book. I love Terriers, and this book is great -- it has tons of adorable pictures. It also has some interesting info about terriers that I never knew. Thanks again,
    Meghan

A thank you note is always appreciated. It is a sign of good manners and consideration.

taste to bring an inexpensive gift, such as some chocolate, or a small plant.

- *If it is raining and you come in wet and dirty . . .* do not just drop your wet things in a pile by the door. Take off your boots so you do not track dirt through the house.

- *Say hello to your friend's parents.* They are people, too.

- *Always ask first.* Before helping yourself from the fridge, using the phone, or wandering around the house, ask the host or his parents for permission.

- *Be courteous during dinner,* and offer to help clean up.

- *Do not be nosy.* It is rude to look in drawers, desks, and cabinets no matter how curious you are.

- *Respect all pets.* If the family has a pet, do not reach out and grab. Be gentle—and ask before petting a dog or a cat.

- *Slumber parties are meant for giggling and talking long into the night,* but remember the other people in the house. Try to keep voices low. If one of the teens wants to go to sleep, her wishes should be respected. The others should either go to another room or talk even lower.

- *Knock before entering the bathroom.*

- *Do not forget to say please and thank you,* especially when it is time to leave.

Pets are "people," too. Be gentle when meeting a dog or cat for the first time. Speak softly and avoid jerky movements. Always ask permission to pet someone else's dog or cat.

- *Show your appreciation by sending a thank you note* after the party or calling the host the next day to tell her what a great time you had.[11]

If a teenager is going to a party that is not a sleepover, the same rules of respect apply. The goal is for a teen to have a good time without embarrassing or hurting anyone, including himself.

Here are some party tricks to try:

- *Get the scoop on the party before the event.* Find out if any friends are going. Have parents make travel arrangements. Figure out what to wear without having to make a mad dash for the store, the dry cleaners, or the sewing drawer.

- *Act like a talk show host.* Regis, Oprah, and Rosie never have a problem talking to people. They make eye contact, smile, and listen. Mingle. Start conversations with a compliment or a question. And do not forget the solitary few who are standing alone. Even if a teen is not the host, a friendly face can go far in making "outsiders" feel comfortable. Remember: Do Unto Others as You Would Have Them Do Unto You.

- *Offer to help.* Bringing out a bowl of chips or a bottle of soda will not take away from any teen's good time.

- *Take a hint.* Even if a teen is having a fabulous time, when a party begins to thin out, that is the cue to leave. Maybe the host's parents want to start cleaning up. Maybe he is tired and wants to go to sleep. The teen should make sure her ride is ready, say her thanks, and go home to sweet dreams of a fabulous time.[12]

Social Whirl # 3: Out on the Town

Dating is probably the most confusing activity of them all. Even adults have trouble with this one. After all, poets and artists have spent centuries trying to figure out what love is all about.

But if a teen develops a romantic crush, confusion will reign. A teen will feel happy one moment, anxious the next. Every action, from a wave in the school hall to a conversation on the phone, will be weighed, analyzed, and discussed with friends and, possibly, parents.

The subject of dating would definitely need more room than the pages of this book, but here is a brief quiz to help teens manage manners in the dating game:

1. *A girl likes a boy so much that when he asks her out, she cannot believe he likes her. She figures . . .*

   a. Her best friend put him up to it.

   b. He is only teasing her.

   c. Maybe he really does like her, and she says yes!

2. *A boy brings his new girlfriend to a dance, but she does not talk to anyone. He figures . . .*

   a. She is not having a good time and is going to break up with him.

   b. She likes someone else.

   c. She is just shy and he has to help introduce her to everyone.

3. *A girl likes her boyfriend very much and she knows that he likes her. But he never asks her to go anywhere. They just talk on the phone. She figures . . .*

   a. He is embarrassed to see her in public.

   b. He really does not like her and he is leading her on.

   c. He is shy, so she has to invite *him* to a movie instead.

4. *A girl is at a party with a guy she really likes. But he keeps trying to kiss her and he is just moving too fast. She figures . . .*

   a. She had better go along with it. Otherwise he will break up with her.

b. She will keep trying to push him away in a friendly manner, hoping he will stop.

c. He is not worth it if he does not take no for an answer. She walks away.

5. *A boy is at his friend's house, when some kids who had also come over get out of hand. They start acting rowdy and sneak in some beer. He figures . . .*

a. He feels uncomfortable but does not want to be a spoilsport. He ignores the situation.

b. He joins in, wanting to belong.

c. He better take his friend aside and discuss the situation with him. It might be time to call in his parents.

6. *A girl really likes a guy, but he does not seem to take the hint. She figures . . .*

a. She will just have to give up on him.

b. He does not like her and, therefore, no one likes her.

c. She will try to get him out of his shell and ask him to join her and her friends at the hamburger place. It is worth a shot.[13]

If teens answer most or some of these questions with the letter c, they are to be congratulated. They already know how to handle themselves before, during, and after a date with poise, grace, and sensitivity. They have a good sense of themselves and are willing to try.

If teens answer any of these questions with an a or b, they need to rethink the difference between cool and uncool. Teenagers feel the push to belong more than adults; they need to be a part of a group.[14] But being a part of the in crowd should never be at the expense of another person's feelings.

"Teenagers can have the confidence to say no," says etiquette expert Ann Nicol. "Once they do, they'll be amazed how easy it can be."[15] If a teen does what is right for her, what she feels comfortable doing, she will gain even more confidence to do it again.

And saying no does not have to be done with a sneer. The same rules of etiquette apply whether it is turning down a beer or a date with someone a teen does not like. Courtesy, sensitivity, and respect almost always work. And, if not, always feel free to leave the situation.

Party and Dating Rules: A Top Ten List

The social whirl of teenagers can be a lot of fun. It can be memorable and entertaining and one and all can have a blast just by following a few simple rules:

Number 10: Plan your party about one month in advance.

Number 9: Mail all invitations! Do not take the chance that an uninvited schoolmate will see a hand-delivered invitation and be hurt.

Number 8: Hosts should be ready about a half hour before the party—and be prepared, too, to greet everyone with a smile.

Number 7: Try to talk to everyone at a party. That includes any shy outsiders who are all alone. If hosting, introduce people who do not know each other.

Number 6: Offer to help serve or clean up.

Number 5: As a guest, be considerate of a host's

property. Do not snoop and do not forget to knock before entering a bathroom.

Number 4: Dress appropriately for the social occasion. Be neat and clean.

Number 3: Be sensitive to a shy friend. If a new boyfriend or girlfriend does not talk much on a date, do not assume it is lack of interest.

Number 2: Always be aware of the other person's feelings, whether on a date or at a party. Be on good behavior and act respectful.

And the *Number 1* rule of party and dating life?

Have the confidence to say no.

Netiquette

*H*ere are some potentially upsetting stories from Suzy Social's files:

- Billy loved his computer. He would turn it on first thing in the morning before leaving for school. After school, he would not turn it off until he had to go to sleep. He stopped watching television. He barely talked to his family at dinner. He was not interested in seeing his friends. All Billy wanted to do was go online. Finally, his parents pulled the plug. Billy had become a computer-holic. He had to "re-enter" the real world, and that meant no computer for two whole weeks.

- Ginny loved e-mailing her friends on the computer. She loved going to chat rooms and talking to other boys and girls about hair and clothes and movie stars. But one night a new person joined in the discussion. He was kind of pushy, immediately asking questions and being nosy. He asked Ginger what she looked like. That raised Ginger's suspicion—and she left the chat room immediately. Ginger was e-smart and did exactly the right thing.

It seemed as if Mark was always in the middle of an exciting computer game when one of his parents would interrupt him with a computer question. At first he felt really cool; his parents were coming to him for advice. But now it was getting on his nerves. He would be short and sometimes downright rude. It was hard being the only computer-savvy person in the family.[1]

There are about 377 million people plugged into the Internet worldwide and their numbers are growing every day.[2] With this kind of popularity, it makes sense that problems would crop up and a whole new set of etiquette rules would have to be created.

Luckily for teens everywhere, those rules have not only been born, they are now etched in cyberspace. Here are some of the e-dos and e-do nots of this computer age.

Chatterbox: Chat Rooms, Discussion Groups, and Instant Messages

A chat room or a discussion group can be a wonderful way to meet new people and learn new things. Discussion groups can help teens find out specific facts for papers they need to do for school. They can also provide advice on hair and makeup and offer tips for the hot new sites online. The familiar beep announcing an Instant Message can also be a welcome chance to chat with a friend and say hello.

But these groups can also be dangerous. Even though a teen is sitting at a computer, hundreds or even thousands of miles away from the person she is talking to, the same old-fashioned rules of safety apply.

Never give out personal information. It is one of the things parents teach their children at a very early age: Do not talk to strangers. Of course, that does not apply to the Internet, where strangers talk and chat and exchange information every second. If anyone starts getting a little too personal on the computer, asking questions about a teen's looks, the person questioned should immediately click off. Never give out phone numbers, addresses, or parents' credit card numbers. Unfortunately, there are "bad apples" out in cyberspace as well as in real life.[3]

Respect the rules. Manners are just as important in the electronic wire world as in the real one. When meeting someone for the first time in a discussion room, a teen should be polite. He should identify himself *by his e-mail name only* and ask what brings the "newbie" into the group. The new person should be given a chance to "speak," to write out his concerns and thoughts. He should not be interrupted while he writes out questions and replies. Some people are slower than others on a keyboard.

Know Thy Site. Most Web sites have sections called "F.A.Q." (for Frequently Asked Questions). A teen should visit the site's F.A.Q. if he is unsure a Web site's discussion group will help him or to see if it is comprised of people with similar likes and dislikes.[4] It can save a lot of wasted time.

Recognize the Instant Messenger. If someone sends an Instant Message (IM) to a teen's computer screen, he

Surfing the Internet is something like racing a car—done solo, but very carefully to try to avoid any unexpected danger—to oneself or the other drivers.

should not answer unless the name is familiar. And if he is busy and does not have time to IM, a polite and quick "Hi! I'd love to chat but I'm swamped. Later!" is perfect netiquette. If a teen is sending an IM to a friend, he should always ask, "Is this a good time? Are you busy?"

We Get Letters: E-mail Etiquette

E-mail is a wonderful invention. Think of it: no postage, no time-consuming longhand letters, and instant delivery. But this fast method of communication can have some drawbacks that a teen should know about before she clicks the "Send" button that delivers the mail.

Faster than a speeding bullet. There is an old expression, "Look Before You Leap." The computer screen might not have a mountainous cliff (unless it is a teen's screen-saver), but the saying still applies. If a friend happens to write an e-mail that sounds angry or upset, the teen who receives it might be angry in turn. Her first impulse would be to write an angry e-mail back. But think back a moment to those old days of "snail mail." It took more than a few minutes to write a letter, lick on a stamp, and take it to the post office. That was enough time for tempers to cool and reason to set in. There is no such luxury with e-mail, and a teen who launches off a nasty note into cyberspace cannot change her mind. (The one exception is America Online. A person can click "Unsend" if the recipient has not yet read it.) Think before replying to any e-mail.

Use spellcheck. Sure, it is easy to send an e-mail. It is almost like doodling. But no one likes to see a messy letter whether in paper or on the net. Before sending an e-mail out into the cyberwilderness, teens and adults alike should check over their notes for spelling, grammar, and punctuation.

Dot every i and then some. E-mail only works if it gets to the person it is meant for. Computers are not post office workers. They do not know that .col is really .com. They do not know that .ort is really .org. If a teen uses the wrong e-mail address, it will either go to the wrong person or be returned as undeliverable. The person who e-mailed not only might be waiting for a reply and wondering what happened, but also the wrong person might be reading his mail.[5]

Protect the privacy of others. People should not give out phone numbers easily. No one should give out someone else's phone number without permission. It is an invasion of privacy. Similarly, someone's e-mail address should be considered a private number. If a teen wants to give out her e-mail address, she should make sure she knows who is getting it. And she should never give out a friend's e-mail address without asking first. When it comes to "forward to" and "copy to" on the e-mail form, a teen should forward mail as blind copies so no one else sees the other e-mail addresses. It is no one's business who gets what when.

Protect personal privacy. If a teen does not recognize an e-mail address, he or she should never open it. Check all new mail entries and delete all the ones that are not familiar so strange ones are not opened even accidentally. Similarly, Instant Messages from people a teen does not know should be instantly ignored.

Netiquette: A Top Ten List

The Internet is an exciting place to be. It can be an invaluable tool for education, for information, and for the exchange of ideas and hints. It also gives a whole new meaning to the word "pen pals." A teenager can e-mail a new friend who lives in Fiji, in Australia, or in her own backyard.

To make the net as civilized, safe, and enjoyable as it can be, teens only have to follow a few simple rules.

> *Number 10:* Check out a discussion room before taking the plunge.
>
> *Number 9:* Create neat, clearly written e-mails.

Use Computer Sign Language Correctly

A teen can sometimes find it a challenge to put the correct emotion in an e-mail. And sometimes she wants to make sure that the message she sends is clear; she meant that comment as a joke or she is really sad about something. To help her out, computer experts have devised sign language to put the e for emotion into e-mail. (But beware. Even symbols can be easily misunderstood. Reread and edit all e-mail before sending it out.)

Some sign language samplings include:

:-)   A smile

:-)))) Lots of laughs

:- (Sad

:-O   Shocked

:- X   Lips are sealed[6]

Number 8: Make sure e-mail addresses are correct.

Number 7: Share computer time with everyone in the family.

Number 6: Be patient with elders. Parents sometimes need help navigating the Internet, and a teen should feel proud that he can provide it.

Number 5: Do not give out other people's e-mail addresses.

Number 4: Do not interrupt other people in a discussion group or chat room. Treat new people with respect.

Number 3: A teen should never give out his password. He should change it often so no one can steal it.

Number 2: If someone gets too personal in a chat room, get out.

And the *Number 1* rule of the Internet?

Have fun. Learn. Discover. (Just do not forget the real world once in a while.)

Chapter Notes

Chapter 1. Why Be Polite?

1. Rebecca Jones, "Denver Proper: Second-and-Third-Graders Learn the Finer Points of Social Life," *The Denver Rocky Mountain News,* November 2, 1998, p. 3D.

2. *The Random House Webster's Unabridged Dictionary,* second edition (New York: Random House, 1997), p. 666.

3. Shery McDonald, "Etiquette Includes Kindness," *The Denver Rocky Mountain News,* December 9, 1998, p. 12D.

4. Laurie Wilson, "The Ministry of Fine-Tuning: Woman Coaches Young People on Points of Culture and Etiquette," *The Dallas Morning News,* August 30, 1997, p. 3G.

5. Mary Mitchell with John Corr, *The Complete Idiot's Guide to Etiquette* (New York: Alpha Books, 1996), pp. 142–144.

Chapter 2. Home Front

1. Nancy Holyoke, *Oops! The Manners Guide for Girls* (Middleton, Wisc.: Pleasant Company Publications, 1997), p. 8.

2. Personal interview with Ann Nicol, January 13, 2000.

3. Ibid.

4. Esther B. Aresty, *The Best Behavior, The Course of Good Manners—From Antiquity to the Present—As Seen Through Courtesy and Etiquette Books* (New York: Simon and Schuster, 1970), p. 50.

5. Zack Elias and Travis Goldman, *How Not to Embarrass Your Kids: 250 Dont's for Parents of Teens* (New York: Warner Books, 1999), p. 11.

6. Letitia Baldrige, *Amy Vanderbilt's Everyday Etiquette* (New York: Bantam Books, 1981), p. 20.

7. Alex J. Parker, Ph.D., *How Rude! The Teenagers' Guide to Good Manners, Proper Behavior, and Not Grossing People Out* (Minneapolis: Free Spirit Press, 1997), pp. 107–108.

8. Ibid., p. 327.

9. Anne Beatty and Ken Dirck, English instructors, West Aurora High School English Project, 1201 West New York Street, Aurora, IL 60506, n.d., <http://www.wahseos.aol.com> (July 19, 2000).

Chapter 3. School Rules

1. Personal interview with Dr. Steven Dranoff, December 15, 1999.

2. Ibid.

3. Steven Dranoff, Ph.D., and Wanda Dobrich, Ph.D., *Respect,* Corporate Matters Productions, Ltd. (Livingston, CMP 1999), video.

4. John E. Meeks, M.D., *High Times/Low Times: How to Cope with Teenage Depression* (New York: Berkley Books, 1989), p. 8.

Chapter 4. Public Scenes

1. A Member of the Aristocracy, *Manners and Rules of Good Society* (London: Frederick Warne & Co., Inc., 1934), pp. 11–12.

2. Ibid., p. 160.

3. Ibid., pp. 261–262.

4. Ibid., p. 154.

5. Yona Zeldis, *Coping with Social Situations: A Handbook of Correct Behavior* (New York: The Rosen Publishing Group, Inc., 1987), p. 4.

6. Judith Ré with Meg F. Schneider, *Social Savvy: A Teenager's Guide to Feeling Confident in Any Situation* (New York: Fireside Books, 1992), p. 115.

7. Ibid.

8. Alex J. Parker, Ph.D., *How Rude! The Teenagers' Guide to Good Manners, Proper Behavior, and Not Grossing People Out* (Minneapolis: Free Spirit Press, 1997), p. 62.

9. Ibid., pp. 63–64.

10. Ré, p. 117.

11. Dr. Richard C. Senelick and Karla Dougherty, *Beyond Please and Thank You: The Disability Awareness Handbook for Families, Co-Workers, and Friends* (Birmingham, Ala.: HealthSouth Press, 2001), pp. 30–33.

Chapter 5. The Social Scene

1. Yona Zeldis, *Coping with Social Situations: A Handbook of Correct Behavior* (New York: The Rosen Publishing Group, Inc., 1987), pp. 53–54.

2. Kelly White, "Ouch! That Hurts," *Girls' Life*, April/May 2000, p. 63.

3. Judith Ré with Meg F. Schneider, *Social Savvy: A Teenager's Guide to Feeling Confident in Any Situation* (New York: Fireside Books, 1992), p. 53.

4. Personal interview with Ann Nicol, January 13, 2000.

5. Nancy Holyoke, *Oops! The Manners Guide for Girls* (Middleton, Wisc.: Pleasant Company Publications, 1997), pp. 14–15.

6. John E. Meeks, M.D., *High Times/Low Times: How to Cope with Teenage Depression* (New York: Berkley Books, 1989), pp. 6–7.

7. Holyoke, pp. 44–45.

8. Dale Carlson and Dan Fitzgibbon, *Manners That Matter for People Under 21* (New York: E.P. Dutton, 1983), pp. 71–72.

9. Ibid., pp. 72–73.

10. Ibid., p. 74.

11. Holyoke, pp. 40–41.

12. Zeldis, pp. 53–54.

13. Bill, Dave, and Michelle, "Baffling Boy Behavior . . . Explained!" *Girls' Life*, April/May 2000, pp. 58–59, 77, 79.

14. Ruth Friedkin, "Teenagers, Parties, and Booze," *The Record* (Bergen County, N.J.), January 14, 1999, p. B9.

15. Personal interview with Ann Nicol, January 13, 2000.

Chapter 6. Netiquette

1. Judith Martin, *Miss Manners' Guide to Rearing Perfect Children* (New York: Atheneum, 1984), pp. 202–203.

2. "How Many Online?" (NUA Internet Surveys, September 2000, <http://www.nua.net/surveys/how-many-online/index.html> (September 20, 2000).

3. Alex J. Parker, Ph.D., *How Rude! The Teenagers' Guide to Good Manners, Proper Behavior, and Not Grossing People Out* (Minneapolis: Free Spirit Press, 1997), p. 389.

4. Ibid., p. 379.

5. Gene Wilburn, "Growing Pains on the Internet," *Computing Canada*, April 12, 1995, p. 9.

6. Parker, p. 384.

Further Reading

Hunter, Sharon, ct al. *Developing Leadership & Personal Skills.* Danville, Ill.: Interstate Publishers, Inc., 1998.

Mitchell, Mary. *Dear Ms. Demeanor: The Young Person's Etiquette Guide to Handling Any Social Situation with Confidence and Grace.* New York: NTC/Contemporary Books, 1994.

Post, Emily L., and Joan M. Coles (contributor). *Emily Post's Teen Etiquette.* New York: HarperCollins, 1995.

Wallace, Carol McD. *Elbows Off the Table, Napkin in the Lap, No Video Games During Dinner: The Modern Guide to Teaching Children Good Manners.* New York: St. Martin's Press, 1996.

Wicks, Louise C. *Good Manners for Young People: How to Eat an Artichoke & Other Cool Things to Know.* Eugene, Ore.: Original PB, 1996.

Internet Addresses

Cyberteens
The No. 1 online community for teens on the Web.
<http://www.cyberteens.com>

Dailystory
Advice for teens by teens.
<http://www.dailystory.org>

Dear Lucie
Advice for teenagers from the syndicated columnist Lucie Walters.
<http://www.lucie.com>

Safeteens
Provides useful tips on how to avoid danger while online.
<http://www.safekids.com/safeteens>

Seventeen
The Web site for the famous magazine. There are articles on style, entertainment, beauty, fashion, and relationships, as well as contests and quizzes.
<http://www.seventeen.com>

Teen Advice
Specialists in adolescence answer questions for teens, on everything from school to dating, family, and friends.
<http://teenadvice.studentcenter.org>

Teen Growth
Gives advice about problems teens may face and discusses topics that are of interest to this age group.
<http://www.teengrowth.com>

Index